THE ART *of* RESULTFUL LETTER WRITING

by Robert Ruxton

SECOND EDITION

Mailbag Publishing Company
Cleveland

INTRODUCTION

THE chapters comprising The Art of Resultful Letter Writing were published originally as a series of articles in *The Mailbag*, a Magazine of Direct-Mail Advertising.

These articles, it will be observed, came from the authoritative pen of Mr. Robert Ruxton, Chief of Copy Staff of one of the great Direct-by-Mail advertising organizations of America.

The principles expounded are being constantly exemplified by the author who maintains a remarkable record of highly consistent results marked at frequent periods by successes that are best described as spectacular and dramatic.

Believing the principles and practices expounded by the author as responsible for his success are worthy of wide circulation in a form that will ensure their easy preservation for reference purposes we have embodied them in this brochure which we present to the business world in the sincere hope that it will prove a constructive business force and aid in the betterment of correspondence and written sales work.

TIM THRIFT
EDITOR, THE MAILBAG

The Art of Resultful Letter Writing

By Robert Ruxton

CHAPTER ONE

IT is worth a great deal of money to know how to write a resultful business letter; I speak from experience, having, as a composer of business letters, unexampled opportunities for seeing just what the right kind of letters are capable of.

For instance, I know of one letter that maintains a business house in New York employing some ten people, and which yields the proprietor, over and above all expenses, an income of approximately one hundred dollars weekly.

I know of another letter that maintains a big collection business in the lower end of Manhattan Island. This business is now run by a woman who inherited it on the death of her husband; absolutely without business knowledge of any kind, she was compelled to lean on this letter for support and its automatic mailing to certain specified lists of people has enabled her to maintain what is a profitable business, and to provide her two sons with a fine education, and a beautiful home in expensive apartments up-town.

These are merely chance recollections of what a *single* letter, used continuously day after day and year after year, is capable of doing, and from this angle I have always been very much impressed with the fact that a single good letter of the right kind, mailed to the right list of people, is frequently worth more to its possessor than a big investment in Government 3 Per Cents.

The writer, in attempting to show how to compose a resultful business letter, will ask that he be acquitted of any idea of personal egotism or personal advertising if he brings the fact rather prominently forward that he has for years been engaged by a great number of business firms in originating letters different to what they were sending out, and designed, of course, to get them bigger business, because this fact has a very large bearing and significance on one point that I desire to make and here emphasize with as much power as I can, and that point is this,—

Exceedingly few of the firms that order letters from me ever dream of sending with the order a copy of the letter-head upon which the letter is to be written and sent out, or a specimen of the envelope in which said letter is to be enclosed.

Here then is a very important clue as to the reason why many good letters fail to get the expected results—the writer simply overlooks the importance of the letter-head on which he writes that letter.

YOUR LETTER-HEAD PHOTOGRAPHS YOU TO THE PROSPECT.

When you send a letter to a man, recollect that you do not go to him yourself, and neither does he come to you. Your personality has no chance to influence the deal. Your office and surroundings have no chance to influence the deal. The only thing that can influence the deal is the *look* of the letter, and what is said in the letter. The average man is well aware of the value of appearances in the climb for business success. He keeps himself dressed well and he keeps his offices and surroundings looking as well as he possibly can because he realizes that these things go a long way in getting and closing business.

It has been said, "Clothes don't make the man," and it has also been said, "The apparel oft proclaims the man." It remained for a Russian philosopher to combine the two maxims when he said, "You are introduced to a man by his clothes and you know him by his character." Keep this maxim in mind when you sit down to write a business-winning letter, remembering its mission is to *introduce* you right to the favorable attention of your prospect; see that this is done by the message being carried on the right kind of letter-head in the right kind of envelope.

The slightest reflection on this subject will show that all a man has to judge you by, in a business solicitation through the mails, is the thing that the postman hands him, representing the envelope and letter-head carrying the business message; these flash through the eye, to the brain, a mental image or photograph upon which the prospect acts. If, in lieu of a letter, you were required to send the business prospect a personal photograph of yourself or of your business offices and surroundings, it is safe to say you would not send a photograph that would either not do you justice or that would actually misrepresent your business, yet this is precisely the thing that a good business firm does when it sends its message out on a poor letter-head.

BUY MENTAL, NOT PRESS IMPRESSIONS.

In London, Paris, or New York there are any amount of men doing business on their nerve—and their letter-head. The financial faker of Wall Street realizes to the full the power, strength and business-winning qualities of the letter-head upon which he writes his message, and it goes out finely engraved or finely embossed on the finest procurable kind of bond paper, enclosed in an envelope that crinkles and crackles like a five-pound Bank of England note. Such a letter conveys an atmosphere of financial strength and reputation that couldn't be got in any other way. Men of this stamp know the value—the commercial value—of the right kind of letter-head and willingly pay from thirty dollars to one hundred dollars per thousand for them because they realize that the engraver or embosser or printer is but the *vehicle* through which they are *buying* favorable *mental* impressions. Does any legitimate reason exist why a reliable, responsible house should use poor letter-heads, and the unreliable, irresponsible house the best letter-heads that are procurable?

In considering a point like this we should bear in mind the historical fact that, although the sway maintained on the mind of Queen Elizabeth by the celebrated Dudley, Earl of Essex, was undoubtedly due to the exercise of his remarkable mental powers, yet he was a firm believer in the value of dress as a supplemental aid to a career, as we see in his reply to his brother, the Earl of Suffolk, who reproved him, saying, "Parts like yours need no such varieties." Dudley replied: "The writing of a clerkly scribe takes not from the wisdom of the epistle, but rather tempts to a frequent perusal thereof. Why should a well-fashioned exterior or a nice casket lessen the value of the jewel within it?"

Following my own mental processes I can personally say that my decisions in all mail-order transactions are swayed very largely by the look and appearance of the envelope and what I take out of it. I class the firm or the writer as good, bad or indifferent after such a scrutiny, and subsequent business relations are naturally strongly influenced by the decision I have mentally reached.

A number of years ago I was handling a business upon which decisions as to cash or credit had to be largely reached by the look of the letter. The credit door was shut to many, and opened to many, and looking back I can recall very few errors of judgment made in the light of subsequent experiences. I remember particularly where a very large line of business hung on the question of extending credit or otherwise. I was called into consultation on the matter, sized up letter-head and envelope, and recommended unlimited credit on the account. I could just *feel* that the firm was right.

RECOGNIZE YOUR PRINTER AS A VALUABLE BUSINESS-GETTING FACTOR.

I personally have always appreciated the value of a first class letter-head and have seen a great many demonstrations of such value. I take long yachting cruises and at times need things that it is not possible to get in out of the way towns or villages and it becomes necessary to send to big centers like Chicago, New York or San Francisco. Frequently the proposed transaction involves a C. O. D., or the shipment of something on credit through the price not being known when being ordered, and it has been my experience that the letter-head carrying the order has been a very important factor in securing the prompt action so earnestly desired.

If this preliminary chapter will make clear the fact that the look, feel and appearance of the envelope and letter-head are frequently equal to a business rating or recommendation it will have accentuated a point that in my opinion has not been accentuated enough in the minds of business men; therefore I have opened this series of articles in the form of a plea or brief for the printer, embosser, engraver and paper maker, asking men who wish to buy good mental impressions to go to such men and procure from them the very best they know how to deliver, simply because it will pay, and will pay big.

In chapters following I will show what principles I follow in the construction of the message that goes on the letter-head, in such fashion, I hope, as will show any man of ordinary ability how to construct a resultful business letter according to principles as final and as fundamental as are the rules of mathematics; I will endeavor to show how to *use* letters to the best advantage and point out errors in circularization that are committed by a great number of business men and which are responsible for an enormous loss annually to the business houses of America.

BOOKS

LIBRARY MATERIAL

INTERLIBRARY LOAN
MAILED UNDER SEC. 34.83 P. L. & R.

To

INTERLIBRARY LOAN DIVISION
HARLAN HATCHER GRADUATE LIBRARY
THE UNIVERSITY OF MICHIGAN
ANN ARBOR, MICHIGAN 48109

MAY BE OPENED FOR POSTAL INSPECTION IF NECESSARY.

EXPRESS COLLECT   INSURED   MAIL

EXPRESS PREPAID   VALUE

From

Form 6298s

CHAPTER TWO

"And shouldst thou ask my judgment of that which hath most profit in the world,
For answer take thou this: The prudent penning of a letter."—Tupper.

IN the previous chapter I laid great stress on the importance of typing the business-winning letter on the right kind of letterhead, and on mailing the right kind of business-winning letter in the right kind of business-winning envelope. I hope the big idea sunk in: *Persuasion* is a big business-winning factor but *Appearance* equals it. A letter swings on just such a see-saw—Persuasion at one end and Appearance at the other. The mistake of most writers is to either give Persuasion more than half the plank or Appearance. In either event the game is spoiled.

Consider the printer, my friends—consider him in his rightful relation to you, provided he is a good printer—a factor and a very important factor in getting you the results you crave, and, in dealing with him, say this to yourself over and over again:

"I am *not* buying press impressions, but I *am* buying mental impressions."

Now, what else makes a letter "Pull"?

The *message* of course.

How are you to get that message?

Precisely as the engineer generates *power*— by concentrating a ton or more of coal under a ton or more of water confined in a boiler to which piston and flywheel and factory are attached.

Turn your *mind* on your business—that's the fire that makes the steam that turns the wheels that make your business *go*.

If you look at your business intently enough you will realize perhaps what you have never realized before—that it is a thing managed by you that is giving a *service* to your fellow men.

And,—

As you look and as you ponder, you will begin to aspire to give a better and more perfect *service*, first because you will realize that your material success hinges on that, and second because you will more or less imperfectly realize that service to the world is the intent of the power that works through you and which men call God.

Some men arrive at true service with their eyes fixed on *profit* while others arrive at profit with their eyes fixed on *service*. The "profit" route is the dangerous way. The service route is the safe way. The man who gives the world service is of use to the world, the world will use him, and, in the process he will profit. The man who takes profit from the world may forget service in the white light of the dollars he takes in.

Why this dissertation?

Simply because I want to impress on you the

fact that I cannot teach you how to advertise your business unless the business is *forcing* you to advertise it. If you don't feel that "urge" you are not looking at your business as you should and *nothing* can make it grow. *A successful business is merely the crystallization of a frame of mind.*

Turn the fire of your mind on your business and advertising power will generate.

And now, about the structure of that letter; your *message* literally glows within you and craves for *utterance;* here's the crucial point; utterance involves technique, and technique the average man lacks.

I once saw a little one act drama; the lover loved as only a lover can—but he couldn't *express* it; when his sweetheart came his very fervor struck him dumb; he lacked the skill to crystallize the words that would reach the brain of his sweetheart through her ear; then came his sweetheart's friend—a sympathetic young girl with the gift of intuition and expression, who, sensing the situation, translated to her companion in eloquent, glowing words the love the lover felt.

Later came the villains, intent on abduction —here the psychical resigned to the physical; *action* was called for and the lover, in his element, *expressed* himself defending his lady-love and her companion against tremendous odds, his good sword finding heart and throat till the attackers lay dead and wounded around him, and he, gasping and fainting from loss of blood, supported at the last by his lady-love madly imploring him to live because she loved him.

And of course he lived.

I often think of that little drama in relation to business—of thousands upon thousands of business men rendering *service* through *action* to a *limited* constituency, powerless to express that service *through words* to the enormously larger constituency just beyond.

The little business or shop, well kept as to windows and stock, is moving in the comparatively little circle bounded by those people who come to or pass that shop—to the greater world beyond those boundaries the proprietor is *dumb*.

Letters *interpret* the business to the larger circle of buyers as the companion interpreted the lover to his mistress, and the man unable to express himself should seek the services of those *who can*—those who, intuitively, sympathetically and skillfully crystallize the ideals of the business into persuasive selling words, and win the heart of the great buying constituency around.

Business consists of men who are *making* goods, *distributing* goods, and *selling* goods. It is wise to determine in which circle you are and to confine your efforts to the business you are in. My province, for instance, throughout my life has been selling goods by the written word. I never attempt to make them. Thousands I know who make goods attempt to sell them. The result is usually disastrous.

From which we may deduce that it is bad for anyone not possessing the faculty of *expression* to attempt a business love-tale to the public. Precisely because men attempt it do they damn letters as resultless.

But,—

If you *do* possess that faculty, go to it— cultivate it—it is a precious jewel worth more to you than your shop, stock and good will, because by its light and glow you will be able to reflect into the other man's mind *new facades of interest* in regard to the commonest things you handle.

Now writers of good letters have, like myself, and with probably better success than myself, attempted to formulate *rules of construction* by the use of which a letter would "pull."

These rules are excellent in their place and I will certainly give them for the benefit of the readers of this brochure, but at best they are an *aid* only to good letter writing, just as the carpenter's rule is an aid only to good construction. A poor carpenter could not proceed without a rule, but a good one could; he would probably make a rule. In other words good letter writing is dependent in the last analysis on *principles*, knowledge, experience and *imagination*.

Those writers who have attempted to formulate rules of letter writing insist for one thing on the importance of a good opening paragraph to gain the requisite ATTENTION. This has its place, and its important place. Speaking personally, however, I may say *the spirit beneath the letter* is the thing that always attracts me. Perhaps I will be better understood if I say the spirit beneath the *letters*—or *words*. The written word is simply the crystallization of some man's *thought* and we place that mentality in the good, bad or indifferent class by what I may term the *look* of the letter—though it is something else beside that.

For instance: a letter reaches me in the mail, or I pick up *The Saturday Evening Post* and glance at an article. In reality my eyes during that brief glance flash a hundred impressions to my brain. I take in the page in a hundred "spots" representing words that stud the page—like flashing jewels, dulled glass, or daubs of clay. My brain is instantly caught by the *radiance* of words or repelled by their lack of it. Great writers intuitively have grasped what is really *the gripping power* in a letter, article, essay or book. I can do no better than quote to exemplify my argument,—

"Words that *speak* and words that *weep*."—*Cowley.*
"There are words that *cut* like steel."—*Balzac.*
"The *artillery* of words."—*Swift.*
"*Razors* to my wounded heart."—*Shakespeare.*
"Words are but *pictures* of our thought."—*Dryden.*
"Some syllables are *swords.*"—*Henry Vaughan.*

Do you see what is meant? A letter may be a model of *construction;* perfect in rule and rote, but it will neither speak, weep, cut nor picture unless, *back of it,* expressing itself in letters, words and syllables on the page before you, is a *mind* of originality, power and force.

And,—

The first thing talent does in writing is to forget rules and methods and pour out its *message* in living, burning words from the heart and from the brain.

Yet, as the student must master the technique of the piano, so the man wishing to learn to write must, first at least, lean on the rules of grammar, punctuation, construction—just in proportion to his genius for the work will he finally pass, outstrip and discard those rules and work to the individuality and power within him that takes him unquestionably and unerringly to RESULTS.

Turn your *mind* on your business—look at it, study it long enough and you will realize that everything on earth has some relation to it and you to it. When the glow comes *expression* will follow—if you have it. If not, the fire of enthusiasm you feel can be translated sympathetically by men who intuitively feel and *can* express what you desire *to* express.

That is the lesson this chapter teaches—the springs of success are within yourself. Begin with that thought. All else will follow. Begin today.

CHAPTER THREE

IN business there are three chief kinds of letters which technically are designated—
(1) "Inquiry-Bringers" or "Canvassing Letters."

(2) "Answering" or "Sales Letters."

(3) "Follow-Up" Letters.

A man manufactures some article that has a limited appeal. Generally he knows that say one out of a group of a hundred people will be interested in what he has. What he has is sufficiently complex and sufficiently costly to be described in a rather expensive booklet. If he has to virtually throw a hundred booklets away to reach *one* buyer his campaign is going to be expensive. To avoid this he keeps the expensive booklets on his shelves and sends out a letter either giving a brief epitome of what the booklet contains, or giving a brief summarization of the goods, offering to send exhaustive details *on request*.

The request sorts out the *one* out of the hundred who is interested. The expensive booklet goes to this name and, possibly, an expensive "Follow up." Perhaps, in the course of years a good deal of money will be spent on that "prospect" and thousands like him who answered the first "Canvassing" or "Inquiry-

Bringing" letter, so the utility of the letter ought to be apparent enough. It has prevented *waste.*

This "Canvassing" or "Inquiry-Bringing" letter has also done something else; it has insured an *attentive* audience. People in this world are apt to *dodge* what you *throw* at them and *catch* what they *ask* you to throw. This is a very important psychological principle to recognize and act upon in all mail order work. The idea in business is not to send a booklet to an uninterested man (he won't read it) but to an *interested* man; he will read it. We have absolutely no chance of converting a buyer who will not read what we write, but a most excellent chance of converting the man who will read the message intended for him.

Nearly all the great advertisers proceed on this principle. They do not send out their booklets indiscriminately to the population of America, but *advertise* their business or their booklets describing it, and form their mailing list of people who have evinced interest by *inquiring.* The man selling a fairly expensive article or service is foolish to waste his printed matter and energies by following a different method—hence the "Inquiry-Bringer"—a letter fulfilling, in the mails, what the advertisement does in newspapers and magazines.

"ANSWERING" OR "SALES LETTERS."

The "Answering" or "Sales Letter," as its name indicates, *answers* the interested *inquiry* (ordinarily a booklet goes with it). It may do one of two things: it may heighten interest in the booklet accompanying it (thus making doubly sure the question of perusal) or it may, in conjunction with the booklet, drive direct for the sale, endeavoring to clinch down the order and get the money there and then. The phraseology and policy of this letter may vary to the above extent, according to circumstances.

"FOLLOW-UP" LETTERS.

Follow-Up letters deal with two classes of people in the main: First, the *obdurates*, who have failed to respond to the first sales letter and booklet; and, second, those delayed in their response by want of the necessary money. Betwixt and between these lie those who were sold but were negligent in buying, and those who were partly sold, but not sufficiently to order.

It is the work of the follow-up to—

(1) Find new arguments to win the orders from the obdurates.

(2) To keep those who intend to order continuously reminded so that when they *can* order they will.

(3) To "ripen" the half-ripened "prospect," deepening and strengthening the original impression created till they are worked up to the buying point.

Understanding now the three most important types of letters we will be better enabled to construct one or more of its peculiar kind, in the most effective way, which means that we will not try to sell with an "Inquiry-Bringer" or procure an inquiry from a "Sales Letter" except to the extent special conditions indicate.

A RULE FOR BUSINESS LETTER WRITING

As a general rule an article fairly high in price cannot be sold through a single letter; this means any price from $1 up.

A low priced article, ranging from a dime to a dollar, may be sold on a single letter.

To both these rules there are exceptions.

The elements of the sale require that—

The "prospect's" *ATTENTION* be gained.

That his *INTEREST* be aroused and *held* till,

We find his *DESIRE* burning strongly to possess, at which time we STIMULATE HIM TO ACTION.

The "Sale," it will be seen, therefore, comprises four steps or stages of mentality through which we must bring the "prospect." We must, before we make the sale, accomplish the feat of making him think in four consecutive directions at certain periods of the sale, and as the sale progresses. If, like the chameleon, his colors changed as his emotions changed we could imagine such a prospect passing successively through shades of White and Red and Blue and Gold, in precise proportion to the extent of our success in passing him through the four stages of "The Sale."

FINDING THE MARKET.

Now the first step in selling is to find a "Possibility." We do not want to deal with "Impossibilities." If I was in New York City with a horse for sale I would endeavor to find men who had horses, or bought horses, or who liked horses, and who, generally, were in a position to house the horse I had.

A man must approximate his market place before he can market what he has; he would be foolish to attempt to sell furs to ladies in the tropics or Palm Beach clothing and underwear to exploring parties bound for the frozen wastes of the north.

Well, I am in New York City with my horse —thoroughbred, we will say, valued at some thousands of dollars. I either find my "possibilities" with a "Canvassing" letter, or reach them through the "Horses and Carriages for Sale" of the *New York Herald*.

Keeping consideration to letters, suppose I went and bought a list of horse owners from a list broker. Those names, if accurate, would be my "possibilities." I send out my "Canvassing" or "Inquiry-Bringing" letter describing my horse in brief, succinct terms, and offer to furnish *full information* to those *interested*. Those interested *reply*. These replies are now my *"prospects."* Those who have not replied do not interest me any more because, manifestly, they are not interested in me, or in what I have.

Now, my horse is worth say $5,000 and I have to get that for him. If I do I make a handsome profit. Possibly I have other horses to sell, "Back on the ranch." Remember, *The Written Word* has to make the sale, or bear nearly its full burden.

Now, the average letter, typewritten and single spaced, contains about three hundred words. When I tell you that a single letter should not be relied upon to make the sale of an expensive article you will begin to see why. Would you attempt to make $5,000 sales in *three hundred words*? Instinctively you would feel you could not do that. If you were a professional business writer your instinct, transmuted to knowledge, would tell you that was not possible, because to make a sale you must pass through the four stages of *Attention, Interest, Desire,* and *Action,* and you know three hundred words is woefully insufficient for that purpose—you know just as certainly as the naval architect knows that he cannot build a hundred foot vessel in a fifty foot building. *There are limitations that bind us mentally just as they do physically,* and the art of mental achievement is to know what time and space we must have to achieve a certain fixed purpose.

Do not confuse the issue in this case. I could of course so describe the horse that an interview would be requested, and, at that interview I could so demonstrate that horse that a sale would be effected. In that case the letters have helped towards a sale but not made the sale itself. The interview and demonstration did that. Letters are frequently used just this way, and this is one of the most effective ways in which letters can be used—to arouse sufficient interest to insure a call, or to be requested to call, replying on subsequent conversation and demonstration to make a sale.

I am assuming, however, that the sale of this horse has to be made without me and the buyer meeting—that title passes eventually through The *Written* Word.

Keeping these factors in mind you will find that while the "Inquiry-Bringing" letter can be short (say one page) the "Sales Letter" must be relatively long (say twenty pages)—please don't gasp, this isn't as bad as it looks when we come to *methods!*

So far, then, we have got a list of "possibilities" made up of, say, 10,000 names. We have canvassed these "Possibilities" with an "Inquiry-Bringing" letter and got, say, ten per cent replies, making a list of one thousand "Prospects." Assuming we have a string of horses perpetually for sale, "Back on the ranch," we then have to see how many of these one thousand prospects we can eventually make *customers and buyers.*

In the process we will use an "Inquiry-Bringer" or "Canvassing" letter (or a *series* of them), a "Sales Letter" (aided probably by a booklet) and a "Follow Up," comprising a

*See concluding paragraphs on last page.

series of letters mailed say ten days apart till exhausted. These are the *Tools* through which we *make* the *Sales*. I sincerely hope that before we get through we will be first-class workmen, able to do creditable jobs of mental carpentering. We will, I hope, get to actual *construction*, with all its rules for architecture, with examples to follow, in our next.

CHAPTER FOUR

I HAVE shown that there are three chief kinds of letters used in business, i. e., "Inquiry-Bringers" or "Canvassing" letters, "Answering" or "Sales" letters, and "Follow-Up" letters.

It may be said that a correct mail-order plan follows the rule indicated by the sequence of the letters; first, it gets the INQUIRY (by the "Inquiry-bringer"), then it attempts the direct sale (by the sales letter) and, if that attempt is not immediately successful, it "Follows-up" by the "Follow-Up" Letter.

To be logical, therefore, we should treat the various groups of letters in their right order, and this of course brings us to a consideration of the "Inquiry-Bringer."

Inquiries are the seed from which spring sales. A good inquiry-bringing letter can easily double or treble the volume of sales by bringing in double or treble the past ratio of inquiries. As we proceed we will see that ALL well written letters (Inquiry-Bringers, Sales and Follow-Ups) are governed by one set of principles in their construction. They must each arouse Attention, create Interest, stimulate Desire, and bring about Action.

To my mind a good letter, accomplishing the purpose for which it is intended, compares in principle exactly with the principle of the wedge, and this may be illustrated as follows, the wedge being the letter itself, and the divisions different parts of that letter.

The opening paragraph is the sharp end of the wedge, representing the Attention section; as perusal proceeds Attention deepens to Interest, then to Desire, and finally, around the last paragraph, to Action.

ACTION

DESIRE

INTEREST

ATTENTION

Let us take a typical "Inquiry-Bringer" and see if we can observe these principles working out in mathematical sequence—the following letter brought forty per cent. inquiries on an investment proposition—an extraordinarily high percentage in a field where the average "Inquiry-Bringer" secures about 2 to 6 per cent. only of inquiries.

Observe how closely the letter follows mentally the "wedge" principle that we illustrate physically. This is one secret of its success.

If the letter is carefully studied *another* secret for its success will disclose itself, constituting a second and very effective principle to use in "Inquiry-Getting" letters, provided it is not carried too far.

I consider this second principle of great importance and I want you, Reader, to *find it yourself*, out of the letter, if you can.

Apart from the construction and wording of this letter, what made it "pull" the inquiries as it did? What factor in human nature was played on so that readers fairly "itched" to answer it? The factor worked upon can be expressed in one word—what is that word? If, after reading the letter, you feel as if *you* would like to answer it and get the reply, ask yourself why. Ask yourself what urge the letter contains to make you feel that way. If you come at the matter this way it is safe to say I will have succeeded in getting a principle of successful letter writing into your mind that you will never forget, but, on the contrary, will use to your profit year after year.

Our next chapter will tell you the second factor that made the letter pull. Try and anticipate that information so that you may compare notes.

Dear Sir:—

Men made iron and steel for many years, yet it remained to the latter half of the nineteenth century to revolutionize the industry and to give growth and multiplication to "A thousand millionaires."

ATTENTION SECTION

Men "In steel" while this magic change was in progress, made fortunes, literally "in a night"; its history has proven a romance of industry.

And it is about to be duplicated—not in steel, but in another industry *that stands in the same position that steel stood half a century ago.*

INTEREST SECTION

It is ripe for revolution—and revolution is upon it—it also will make "A thousand millionaires."

Today it presents one of the most promising openings for capital—large or small—it is possible to conceive.

The conditions governing it are—extraordinary—unique—its promise is spectacular—it will not alone duplicate, but *exceed* the marvelous record of steel.

DESIRE
SECTION   May we tell you more about it?

You can share with us in the rewards just ahead.

ACTION   We have prepared a brochure for *limited distri-*
SECTION   *bution* among men we believe will be interested in
the FACTS; it is expensive, and we do not wish to
mail it to you without the assurance that it will be
at least READ. If you would like to read it, and will
make request on enclosed postal, this brochure will
be mailed to *you entirely without expense or obligation.*

May we send it?

Very truly yours,

It will be perceived that the *object* of this
letter was not to make a sale but to produce an
inquiry. In producing an inquiry that ulti-
mately turned to a sale the letter became of
course part of the sales campaign, and of course
the ultimate sale was its final objective. The
important thing to grasp here is that the act
of selling to a man buying is arrived at by a
series of steps not usually apparent to the
buyer, and sometimes not even apparent to
the seller. Many salesmen are splendid result-
producers yet cannot tell exactly *how* they
make their sales. If their methods are examined,
however, it will be seen that they all, by different ways, methods, manners and ideas, pass
the "prospect" through the stages of Attention,
Interest, Desire and Action, "Closing" when, in
their judgment, they have the man before them
at the final stage.

The reader may be interested with a bit of
history connected with this letter and the
material that followed it. The man that
ordered it had *a big idea*, but nothing in the way

of assets; he had, in fact, hardly sufficient capital to pay for the material he ordered. The letter, as previously stated, proved remarkably successful in bringing in the *inquiries* from the right class of people (carefully selected in advance.)

The writer received a letter from him some time later containing the following extracts:

"I am writing this letter to you personally as I desire at this time some advice as to my future plans. * * * I want to say I have succeeded in placing practically all the issue of bonds at par. This will enable the —— factory to fully carry out their plans to install their plant and will also enable the writer to retain 98 per cent. of all the stock.

* * * * I found it an advantage to have more than one kind of bond to handle. I saw an opportunity to purchase a telephone company at much less than the actual value of the plant. I purchased this with a cash expenditure of a few thousand dollars, bonding it for enough to completely pay for the company, sold the bonds above par so as to net the telephone company par, and now own the telephone company clear, all out of debt, and have $10,000 cash for the extensions—this all secured by means of the bonds issued on the telephone plant."

Thus this man, with but a few hundred dollars capital (sufficient to pay for the presentation literature), found himself almost over night made wealthy and independent through the power of a few letters and a booklet! The original success turned his head; he went into promotion work on a diversified scale, cutting himself off from information or advice, and achieved, on the reputation of his original success, other successes which turned to failure through rank inexperience, and he died, eventually, a disappointed, broken man in an obscure mining camp—not the first time by any means that I have seen a man go down to ruin through a success achieved *too easily* and too suddenly by a series of well planned letters and booklets.

In the next chapter we will make reference to this letter again and you will probably be interested in studying it anew in the light of information and knowledge yet to come.

CHAPTER FIVE

Curiosity is lying in wait for every secret.—Emerson.
Curiosity is as much the parent of attention as attention is of memory.
—Whately.
The first and simplest emotion which we discover in the human mind is curiosity.—Burke.

IN the last chapter I introduced a typical "Inquiry-Bringer" and illustrated the physical, psychical and mechanical principles (order and sequence of ideas) through which it was made productive (for, be it remembered, this letter went through the fire of experience and trial and proved extraordinarily productive).

We find such a letter is a mental *wedge*—that it plays on the mind of the "prospect", putting him alternately into mental conditions of Attention, Interest, Desire and Action—these are the principles and motives that move him to *Act* on receiving and reading that letter.

I stated there was another motive in which the four named were bathed, as it were, and asked my readers to express *that* motive by a single word—that word is—*curiosity.*

Read the letter again and you will see it lacks a positive subject—we explain the properties of a thing without saying what the thing itself is. In a sense the letter is an interesting conundrum that it is to the *interest* (through the Desire section) of the reader to have solved. His only method of getting the answer is to *write*—hence 45 per cent did write.

Curiosity is a two-edged sword; like all other forces it must be used with great care and discrimination; in its place, under right conditions, it is exceedingly effective. In this case the letter did not seek to provoke the curiosity of everyone indiscriminately; on the contrary, it was mailed to a carefully *selected* list of names from every one of which it was most desirable to receive the reply that indicated the necessary *attention*.

The letter in reply deepened attention to interest and conviction and the order was landed because we had taken care that when we had a *convinced* man we also had a man of sufficient *means* to put up the sum asked from him.

Working on picked lists of names the principle of CURIOSITY can be legitimately and effectively employed as the first step in mail salesmanship. The same principle might be disastrous if employed indiscriminately on a newspaper or magazine advertising campaign, flooding, as it would do, the sponsor with a mass of undesirable inquiries.

The principles of Attention, Interest, Desire and Action have been pretty well expounded by others in the past, though I hope to have something new to say about them before I have finished, but the principle of CURIOSITY has not been explained as it should, because, perhaps, it has not been perceived in its true relationship as "The parent of Attention."

If space permitted I could here stop and write chapter after chapter rich with citation and example on this CURIOSITY theme alone and I could tell some extraordinary instances of prolific results accruing from it when judiciously and intelligently used. Space is strictly limited, however.

A few illustrations may be permitted; take gold—it is an extraordinary metal—a paradox. In times of panic when all other values fall its value *rises*. The world has never had enough of it, and cannot get enough of it; it is free from competition; patents and inventions cannot hurt it, monopolies cannot "corner" it, and it is good throughout the world, in any shape or form, provided it is pure, for things that no other things could exchange for.

Take "Gold" out of that sentence and you have a "Conundrum" letter that, linked with a gold mine, makes it look distinctly to the reader's interest to solve by replying and reading the answer to his reply.

If that reader was a known buyer of gold mines, or of mining shares, you have gripped his *attention* by a method that is not ordinarily followed, and, provided skill and ability is used after that stage, results must be in exact proportion.

———

We pick up a letter physically and mechanically right—it is shaped like a wedge and we can trace (as per example given) the various *steps* from Attention to Action.

This, according to the critics, might constitute an exceedingly good letter; as a matter of fact, it might be an exceedingly bad letter; it is one thing to mix a dish up from the proportions given in a cook book, but quite another thing to bring out of the pot or oven the thing of flavor and savor it was designed to be.

Various writers on the subject of letter writing have (and rightfully) placed great stress on the opening paragraph. My own method, in determining whether I consider a piece of printed matter worthy of the time necessary to take for perusal, is to "sample" it, quickly and thoroughly, in a score of places. The man who had an ingenious "Opening paragraph" would get my attention for a second of time and lose it a few seconds after did not my test reveal a continuous thread of cleverness and thought throughout what he had written.

I arrive at decision, I have found, by what I may term "stabbing" the manuscript or letter with my eyes; in other words I pick out, with lightning-like rapidity, bits of the Mss. "five words long" that literally "bleed" (or otherwise) with thought as I pounce.

I do this consciously—the average man does it unconsciously; if the words are mediocre, drab and dead, down goes the Mss.—down and out so far as I am concerned. If, on the other hand, I find something approximating Tennyson's specifications,

> "*Jewels five-words-long*
> *That on the stretch'd forefinger of all Time*
> *Sparkle forever.*"

Then I am interested—then that Mss. goes either into my pocket for leisurely perusal, or into an arm chair with me for instant reading. The information of a letter is one of its points of contact with the human mind, but its success lies,—not with its information, nor with its opening nor closing paragraph, but in the sustained skill and thought throughout it, on *the* page, in *the* paragraphs, in *the* sentences, and sections of sentences "five words long."

This fact explains why what seems to be an extraordinarily bad letter from the standpoint of the "Experts" will still produce extraordinary results. It is a fact that the *writer* of a letter, intensely in earnest, will violate all rules of construction and have its presentation topsy turvy, and it is also a fact that the *reader*, gripped by the earnestness, will *mentally reconstruct the letter* and give it its right *setting and sequence*. That both parties act subconsciously and without conscious knowledge of what they are doing mentally in no wise alters the fact that it is done.

In the light of all this we may draw a few helpful conclusions I think, the first being that no man in whom earnestness and enthusiasm burns need despair of being a good letter writer simply because he lacks a knowledge of the technique of the art, and I think we may as fairly conclude that if we can take this earnest, enthusiastic man and give him a knowledge of the technique of the art his *results* will triple or quadruple.

Now what, in the last analysis, makes for earnestness and enthusiasm? Simply the consciousness of being enabled to render a fellow-being *service*. The man with a thing that saves the world time, or labor, or money, is a man working a great economic benefit—he can teach us do things better, cheaper, faster.

Bring this man opposite *another man*—a cynic if you please, and watch him warm up and tell and demonstrate what he has till he has the other fellow convinced in spite of Hell. Why? Because a living, breathing *man* is before him into whose face and eyes he can look and watch and be stimulated by the effect of his words as mirrored in the other's countenance.

Take our service man away and place him opposite a typewriter, a blank sheet of writing paper, carbon paper, and an envelope, and watch what happens; his *eyes* see *material* where before they saw spiritual things; he is no longer faced with flesh and blood and heart and brain and soul and spirit but with cold, immobile *dead* things—he is *demagnetized*.

Yet, through and by these things he must achieve the miracle of personality—he must learn to sway a thousand or a hundred thousand minds precisely as he swayed that *one*—this he must do if he has to spread his message broadcast by means of *the mails*—this he must do if he wants to achieve in a year what would represent a century of time under other conditions—this he must do, and *can* do, if within himself he has that rare, fine, ethereal quality termed IMAGINATION that,—

"Gathers up
The undiscovered Universe,
Like jewels in a jasper cup."

We will, in our next, take up this great subject in the hope that we may find new and useful things that will assist us in the art of resultful letter writing.

CHAPTER SIX

Imagination is the eye of the soul.—Joubert.
The soul without imagination is what an observatory would be without a telescope.—Beecher.

IMAGINATION has two qualities—it enables us to *see* the thing we *think* of, and it enables us to endow the things we see through our material eyes with qualities that others may not see; the latter faculty may perhaps be classed as the finer form of imagination termed Fancy and we find it predominating in poetic imagery. In the words of Fuller, "Most marvelous and enviable is that fecundity of fancy which can adorn whatever it touches, which can invest naked fact and dry reasoning with unlooked-for beauty, make flowerets bloom even on the brow of the precipice, and when nothing better can be had, can turn the very substance of rock itself into moss and lichens. This faculty is incomparably the most important for the vivid and attractive exhibition of truth to the minds of men."

It may seem a strange assertion that the faculty of the poet should have a use—a vital-constructive use—in prosaic business, but it certainly has. A gasoline engine, for instance, to the manufacturer is apt to be but a thing of iron and steel and brass and babbitt, wrought out by mechanical processes in a noisy, smoky factory at the cost of so much tabulated time and labor and money.

A yachtsman may look at that engine in an entirely different light; he conceives it wrought under Thor-like hammers into a thing of grace, and beauty and strength.   To him it becomes something almost sentient—a faithful *friend*, that, when howling gale and breaking seas threaten his destruction, hums cheerily beneath his feet a symphony that breathes of rugged virility and power and dependability—he feels the throbbing, pulsing, vibrant *strength* that is forging him through rushing walls of water towards the haven ahead and when "She" takes him past the breakwater into harbor his feeling approximates sheer *affection*.   An advertisement shot through with the gold of such imagination must necessarily contain qualities that unimaginative announcements lack.

To the grown-up the woods at night—are the woods at night.   But what of the child? To the budding boy or girl in whose mind imagination has woven its magic threads those woods abound in sprites, fairies, imps and gnomes who, in glades glamored by the moon above, give rein to their impish, elfish tricks.

Imagination enables us to conjure up things we *have* seen but do not see now (with material eyes) and make them live again, vivid and real and actual, and it also enables us to take the things we see and give them properties or qualities the unimaginative do not see.   I will point out the value of the first quality in the work of letter writing directly; as regards the second quality it must be plain that the faculty is of tremendous advantage because, possessing it, we can not alone make *ourselves* see what we conjure up, but *others also*.

Imagination, in its finest form, is a constructive force in the work of the world because it dowers logic and reason with a sub-normal sense that carries it past its own limitations into a still greater sphere. Many scientists and inventors have achieved their ultimate goal through pushing reason and experiment to the utmost limits and bridging the gap with imaginative power that *saw* things that *did* exist, but which imagination alone made plain.

A writer capable of self-analysis can observe himself working *in pictures* that flash before his mind like those thrown on the screen by the cinematograph and which he transfers to paper by the symbols called *words* and his power as a writer is gauged in precise degree by his power to make those symbols he puts down *flash back* to the brain of *the reader* those pictures that have passed before his brain. The best results, from writer and reader, come when *both* have the faculty of imagination, therefore; some men lack it, and these men, whatever their other qualifications, can never become either good writers or good readers; it takes an imaginative man to read and appreciate Shakespeare or other great poets.

Imagination, we have found, is a useful tool in business writing; if you aspire to success in this field you must either have it, or you must cultivate it. Read the following words; if they conjure up pictures, scenery, ocean sky and beach and cliff in your mind, then you *have* imagination.

"Sunset and evening star,
And one clear call for me
And may there be no moaning of the bar,
When I put out to sea,
But such a tide as moving seems asleep,
Too full for sound and foam,
When that which drew from out the boundless deep
Turns again home."

Given that first line, if an artist, could you sketch a picture from it? Do you see that picture now?

Again:—

"And the stately ship glides on
To its haven under the hill
But oh for the touch of a vanished hand,
And the sound of a voice that is still."

Take the simple child-song and see how it abounds in *pictures*:

"The sun is careering
In glory and in might,
'Mid the deep blue sky
And the cloudlets white.
The air and the waters
Dance, glitter and play,
And why should not I
Be as merry as they?"

Do *pictures* flash through your mind as you read those lines? Do *you* see what the writer *saw*, reduced to word symbols, and endeavored to *flash back* to *your* brain? If you do, you have imagination.

Take your wife—can you see her now? Not think of her, but actually *see* her as you left her this morning? Can you *see* the breakfast table as you came to it? Can you *see* the parlor of your home—the interior of your church—the face of your friend? All right, you can; then *talk* to him of something mutually known that is of mutual interest. Now, can you see his *expression* change as you talk, now attentive, now sympathetic, now eager? Can you see his eyes light with the spirit of fun, or mischief, or adventure? If so, you have *Imagination* and it is strong or weak in precise degree to the clearness or otherwise of the objects you take to try these tests on.

I wound my last chapter up with these words: "Bring this man opposite *another man* and watch him warm up and tell and demonstrate what he has till he has the other fellow convinced in spite of Hell. Why? Because a living, breathing *man* is before him into whose face and eyes he can look and watch and be stimulated by the effect of his words as mirrored in the other's countenance.

"Take this man and place him opposite a typewriter, a blank sheet of paper, and an envelope, and watch what happens; his eyes see material where before they saw spiritual things; he is no longer faced with flesh and blood and heart and brain and soul and spirit, but with cold, immobile *dead* things—he is *demagnetized*."

But not if he possesses *Imagination*. Through that precious faculty, "The eye of the soul," he *still* faces a human being and as he *talks* to him through writing symbols he can watch his expression change as he brings him through the stages of Attention, Interest, Desire and Action. Imagination has *transformed* a purely mechanical rule or principle into a thing of pulsing life and we deal again, in the solitude of office or den, with living men and women.

Now perhaps you see the tremendous value of Imagination in advertising—you see the faculty of the poet is also the faculty of the plain prose business writer, and, realizing that truth, you will be better able to appreciate those words of Arthur Brisbane, who said:

"The ancient poet was a troubadour, telling the story of his hero in rhyme.

"The modern poet is the advertising writer, telling his story in plain prose, as a rule, realizing that truth *poetically told* is what makes business and success.

"Mr. Business Man, why do you admire certain great figures in history?

"You admire them because of what *able writers* have told you about them.

"If you expect the world to admire *you*, patronize *you*, regard *your* energy, and make *you* rich, you must have *an able writer to tell about you*, and he must be an advertiser who understands the *poetry* of business as well as the commonplace prose of business—one who can give the whole buying world a just estimate of your value and what you are doing."

I have indicated the business value of that phase of imagination that can conjure up a thing or a person seen or known in the past and bring that thing or person into the living present; Mr. Brisbane in the above words indicates the value of that phase of imagination that "Adorns whatever it touches   *   *   *   with unlooked for beauty."

This has its dramatic side; a man starts in business; he lacks capital; energy and ambition take the place of it; he fights a losing battle against the forces of giant competition marketing against him by sheer weight of money; our young business man is *poor* but imaginative,—

> *"When I could not sleep for cold*
> *I had fire enough in my brain,*
> *And builded with roofs of gold*
> *My beautiful castles in Spain."*

And, if his thoughts and tendencies run to advertising, his genius will find in the coldness and deadliness of business poverty the brain-fire that will build figments of imaginative thought into the product he makes, showing qualities that are there, but which ordinarily are not seen, in a light that will cause them to glitter and glow and *attract*.

That man will give prosaic things like soaps and powders and fabrics a halo of fancy that will endear them to the hearts of millions and bring them into millions of homes, lifting him to the golden throne of independence and wealth in the process.

CHAPTER SEVEN

While fancy, like the finger of a clock,
Runs the great circuit and is still at home.—Cowper.

Mine eyes he closed, but open left the cell of Fancy, my immortal sight.—Milton.

Imagination, where it is truly creative, is a faculty and not a quality; it looks before and after, it gives the form that makes all the parts work together harmoniously toward a given end, its seat is in the higher reason, and it is efficient only as a servant of the will.—Lowell.

IN our previous chapter I dwelt upon the importance of imagination in letter writing and demonstrated, I hope, the general method of application. Now for concrete instances; in explaining this phase of our subject I naturally cannot enter into and describe the thoughts and feelings of other men, so, to be accurate, I am forced to analyze and describe my own. In view of this fact I hope the reader will forgive any apparent egotism in the understanding that the treatment of the subject renders necessary the pronoun "I."

Now, when I sit down to write a letter I have a *subject* which may be books, medicines, instruments, tools, money, stocks, bonds, promotions, filters, gloves or anything else.

I propose to talk that subject to thousands of persons by medium of the letter I am to write. My first step is to ascertain as nearly as I can from the *attributes* surrounding the subject (price, quality, etc.), the *type* of man or woman it would appeal to most; I thus get a composite person. I am no longer talking to thousands.

of people but to someone representative *of* those thousands.

Having got my composite person fairly well fixed in my mind I next run back over the list of actual persons I know or have known and select the one that approximates closely in characteristics to the composite person drawn. The latter is then dropped from my mind as the artificial thing it is and I am face to face with *a living man* (or woman).

SELLING THE HARDWARE MAN.

Back in a little seaport town in New York lives a shrewd, close-buying, intelligent hardware man through whom I have often bought. He doesn't buy "shoddy" stuff; he has in fact a remarkable knack of getting the top best the market affords at the lowest price; he is in effect, and in his line, a natural servant to the hardware buying public. He justifies his existence and earns his profits.

Now, when I have *the right kind* of hardware proposition to write about I conjure up Charlie Best (that isn't his name of course) and run *hard facts* into his brain for five minutes. I *see* the effect of my arguments, and I know if I have presented the thing right he will motion for an order blank without saying a word. If I don't see him do that the letter is ripped up and I write and write till I do.

SELLING THE DOCTOR.

In a wealthy suburban town on the outskirts of New York the wants of the community are ministered to by a physician of whom it can first be said he is a gentleman, by birth and breeding, in the true sense of the term. Dr. James (the name will serve) keeps abreast of the latest discoveries and developments in his profession, and, when something really worth while comes out, he has the money to buy, possessing as he does a very enviable practice. If I have medical apparatus or service to sell I conjure up Dr. James and (provided I am personally convinced of the worth of what I have —to him) do not stop till I have his check.

I know just how to talk to the Doctor; he is a finely educated physician, a profound student of psychology, and an appreciative reader of the great poets. There is a touch of the mystical in his nature and I can win his instant attention by striking one of the keynotes that characterize his lines of thought. He is representative of thousands in his class and when I sell him I know I have sold *hundreds with him.*

SELLING THE HOUSEWIFE.

Down in Maine there lives a shrewd little woman who, as the mother and manager of a family of five, limited by an income small, as incomes go, *knows values thoroughly,* and knows when she has a bargain and when she has not. Verbiage won't have any effect on Mrs. Smith (which name will serve) and if by any misrepresentation you succeed in getting goods within her doors not up to value you may expect them back the next day.

Mrs. Smith is a buyer for the cheaper grade of goods *that wear*—she is typical of hundreds of thousands of families and I know when I have sold *her* I have sold a very large proportion of others like her.

SELLING THE BUYER OF BOOKS

In Bridgeport, Conn., lives Ralph (which isn't his name) an erstwhile college boy, now approaching thirty, yet with lots of boyish tricks about him reminiscent of old college days.

Ralph writes little amateur poems, dramas, etc., and is studying literature. He is naturally a book lover, so, when I have a book or books to sell my first task is to make the sale to Ralph; it would be easy if he had the money, but he isn't blessed with a great share of that commodity; however, given the right book and the right talk, he is almost a certain victim on the "Dollar down and a dollar a week" plan, so when I have an installment proposition on books my mind hies forth to Ralph because I know when I have sold him I have sold hundreds of his type.

SELLING THE SPECULATOR.

Down South I have *a speculator* (he would hate to be called that, but he is). He considers himself an investor; the only trouble with that adopted definition is that Charlie's "investments" all stand in to pay him (on their own showing) thousands per cent if he wins. Occasionally he does, and the winners have so far kept him sufficiently well ahead of the game to be able to "plunge" when any good looking venture comes along. Charlie isn't a "sucker" by any means. He is simply that type of business man that balances chances and is willing to take one personally if they seem to favor him or the project he goes into. You would waste time talking "hot air" to Charlie, but take him *a sound idea* and he's "In on it."

When I have a speculative proposition upon which I have myself been convinced I conjure up Charlie and lay it before him; his type is numerous, and when I have him sold I have hundreds of thousands sold.

SELLING THE BANKER.

Down in the New York financial district in "The little crooked street with a graveyard at one end and a river at the other" waiting for the unfortunates who face grim Despair within its boundaries, a great banker has offices. His hobby is automobiles. He wants and will have, if money can buy it, the automobile that is king of the road. If I have that type of automobile to sell I naturally and automatically conjure him up because he is representative of a thousand and one millionaires who buy with him.

So the list runs; over a period of twenty years I have met so many men of special types and characteristics that it has become easy to pick out from those I know the *one man* to whom the proposition will especially appeal.

That man, on each proposition, I pick out and write *to* and *at*. I am opposite to him in his home or office as I write, by and through that gift or faculty of imagination which Washington Irving classed as: "The divine attribute that is irrepressible, unconfinable; that when the real world is shut out can create a world for itself, and with necromantic power conjure up shapes and forms and visions to make solitude populous."

FROM PHANTASY TO REALITY

What is there to it? I do not know! I can only say that this is my method, and through that method I have achieved results—sometimes wonderful results. I have imaged a great life insurance company and watched it assume physical form and actuality from the mists of erstwhile fancy. I have screened on my brain the picture of a great factory through the doors of which poured hundreds of men who set in motion whirring machines—and saw the thing grow as I rubbed the magic lamp! I have visioned a great magazine sending words of comfort and cheer to thousands of hearts sheltered beneath old rooftrees—and saw the thing done even as I thought!

I have seen three hundred thousand dollars worth of automobiles swept off the sales floor within a week by men to whose brains I had flashed *a picture* of the machine that appealed to them and I have seen factory and office powerless to cope with the flood of orders engendered through the faculty to accurately *vision* the type and class of men who would buy on a certain appeal.

THE MESSAGE'S THE THING.

What I have, and what I know, is given as fully and as freely as it has been tendered to me, and I am glad if, as a result of these chapters on the wonder-worker, IMAGINATION, I am able to set the feet of others on the road to success through the art of resultful letter writing.

What I have done I have always felt should have been done, and the wonder to me is that I have never wondered at what came—I have accepted results as the inevitable consequence of certain prior acts and would have felt natural laws had played me false if those results had not come.

It should not of course be thought that the results accomplished in specific cases have sprung absolutely and entirely from the letter, as the term is narrowly understood, though the letter (or letters) have formed, in their letter form, an important and essential part of the campaign. I consider an enclosure, folder or booklet *an extension of the letter proper*, precisely as the telescope is an extension of the faculty of sight.

Primarily and basically a man is reached and influenced through *a message* conveyed to him through the mails, and that *message* is essentially the same whether in the form of a letter of twenty-five pages, or a letter of one page and a related booklet of twenty-four pages that *extends* the letter in the more convenient form of a booklet.

Some day, I hope, I will be privileged to present to the readers of *The Mailbag* the ideas, principles and methods I use in *extending* the letter into accompanying booklet, that of course presupposing a series of articles on the preparation of that very important advertising device —the booklet itself.